AF413380

the beginning of self

INTRODUCTION

I Love Myself, I Love Myself, I Love Myself, I Love Myself, I Love Myself, I Love Myself, I Love Myself, I Love Myself, I Love Myself, I Love Myself, I Love Myself, I Love Myself, I Love Myself, I Love Myself, I Love Myself, I Love Myself.

It took me saying these very words out loud over 10,260 times before I actually loved myself.

I started January 1, 2016 and finally felt like I loved myself May 28, 2017.

I believe this process will work for you too. Maybe you will arrive there faster than me, or perhaps you may need a few extra repetitions. Whatever the case may be just keep going.

The 'I Love Myself', exercise mixed with the other exercises in this book are my daily recipe to maintain and increase my self Love. There is an infinite capacity of Love in the universe and with commitment, an open heart, and an open mind we can continue to grow and expand our Love forever.

The writing of this intro is March 1, 2024 and I can say with confidence 'I LOVE MYSELF', and have since that day in May 2017.

I feel strongly I am able to stay in the space of Love because I have committed to daily doing the exercises in this book. I will continue to do these exercises daily because they work.

Thank you for joining me on this adventure of self Love. I am grateful to share these exercises with you and I look forward to living a life of love and above together.

Love is The Answer! So, let's begin!

Peace
Love
Happiness
Infinite Abundance
--I am

a

attitude

i choose a loving attitude

action: smile + say "i choose love" 10 times

song: ♥only love is real♥ mc yogi

book: ♥the tao of pooh♥ benjamin hoff

quote: love is a choice and i choose love

☮♡☺♥♥★

b
breath
i inhale light
i exhale love

action: inhale light +
exhale love
10 times

song: ♥breathe deep♥
mc yogi

book: ♥breath♥
james nestor

quote: breath is the
currency of
consciousness

☮ ♡ ☺ ♥ ♥ ✦

C

confidence

i know love can

do

all things

action: smile + say "i know love can" 10 times

song: ♥i believe♥ soja + michael franti

book: ♥courage is calling♥ ryan holiday

quote: i can do all things when i choose love

☮ ♡ ☺ ♡ ✱

determination

i choose to allow
love to guide the
way

action: smile + say
'love leads the way'
10 times

song: ♥we will shine♥
mc yogi

book: ♥mastery♥
robert greene

quote: when i follow
love
i succeed at
all i do

☮ ♡ ☺ ♥♥ ✶

exercise

my body is a
temple
i love my
body

action: 15 min answer workout with trainer joe

song: "standing outside the fire"
garth brooks

book: "the rise of superman"
steven kotler

quote: i love my body, and its divine intelligence

F

faith

Love;
a truth desired around
the universe we all
share together

action: put hands on heart + say 'i believe in love' 10 times

song: ♥one day♥ matisyahu

book: ask + it is given esther + jerry hicks

quote: focus = faith

g
gratitude

an attitude of
gratitude
amplifies the feelings
of love

action: thank 1 or more 'strangers' a day

song: ♥kind + generous♥
natalie merchant

book: halleluja anyway
anne lamott

quote: please,
thank you,
i love you,
all i need to
say
☮♡‥˅˅⚹

h

help others

helping others is
love
in action

action: thank 1 or more people from your past who helped you

song: ♥thank you for loving me♥ bon jovi

book: ♥big potential♥ shawn achor

quote: everyone you help is someone's daughter or son. so help everyone.

imagination

action: imagine world love
+ tap your third eye
10 times

song: ♥imagine♥
eva cassidy

book: ♥acres of diamonds♥
russel conwell

quote: the image in the
minds eye
is the reality
experienced by
you + i.

☮ ♡ ☺ ♥ ✳

joke

i have the ability to
find love
every day
+
in every way

action: ___ say 'i am joyful'
10 times daily

song: ___ ♥electric love♥
borns

book: ___ ♥the lion tracker's guide
to life♥
boyd varty

quote: ___ a smile
is the universal
language of
love

🙂 ♥ ♡ ♥ ✶

k

kindness
is
love
in
action

action: say something kind
about yourself
out loud

song: ☮♡☺
G. love

book: the only prayer you
need
debra engle

quote: kindness
is a
choice,
choose
kindness
it makes a difference

Love

the multipule of
acceptance
+
appreciation

action: say outloud "i love my body" 10x

song: ♥love remains♥ kevin paris

book: ♥help. thanks. wow.♥ anne lamott

quote: i want love
you want love
let us be love

m

manifest

may love
be the motivation
of all of
your desires

<u>action:</u> write 'i create love' 10 times

<u>song:</u> ♥"can't stop the feeling"♥ justin timberlake

<u>book:</u> ♥ love + creation ♥ paul selig

<u>quote:</u> when we focus on love, we create + attract more love

n

nutrition

choose nutrients that fill your mental, physical, spiritual, + emotional body with love

action: before each meal or snack say, "thank you body, i love you"

song: ♥nutrition rap♥
andy horne

book: ♥grain brain♥
david perlmutter m.d.

quote: nutrition is food, drinks, people, places + things. choose nutrients filled with love.

open minded

an open mind +
an open heart
are the gateway to
infinite love

action: tap the head + the heart 10 times

song: ♥heaven is here♥
mc yogi

book: ♥siddhartha♥
hermann hesse

quote: an open mind leads to an open heart, an open heart connects us to pure, infinite love

p

purpose

do all things with
love,
and your
purpose
will be
fulfilled

☮ ♡ ☺ ♥ ★

action: say 'my purpose is to love + be loved' 10 times

song: ♥born for this♥ the score

book: ♥awaken your inner fire♥ heather ash amara

quote: at the origin of all purpose is love

☮ ♡ ☺ ♥ ✿

quiet time

quiet the mind,
find stillness with thebody,
tap into the
infinite love

action: +15 min of yin yoga daily (see trainer joe)

song: ♥hallelujah♥ lindsey stirling

book: ♥meditations of marcus aurelius♥ marcus aurelius

quote: love can be found in all places especially in the space in between movement + noise

☮ ♡ ☺ ♥ ★

r
read
what our eyes see and
our ears hear,
quickly become
our life
experiences.
choose love

action: _____ write "i love
myself" 10 times

song: _____ ♥hall of fame♥
the script

book: _____ ♥how i built this♥
guy raz

quote: _____ what you see
you vizualize.
what you hear
you say,
what you read
you think
choose love♥
☮♡☺♥★

S

sleep

When focused on
love,
sleep becomes
second nature

☮ ♡ ☺ ♥ ✲

action: draw 10 hearts before bed ♡♡♡♡♡♡♡♡♡♡

song: ♥ 432 hz ♥ download some

book: ♥ why we sleep ♥ matthew walker

quote: the last thought before sleep, is the first thought when we wake choose love

☮♡ :" ☺♥♥ ✱

t

touch

the power of love
is amplified
with the gift of
touch

<u>action:</u> give your self a hug for 5 breaths

<u>song:</u> ♥look for the good♥
jason mraz

<u>book:</u> ♥the little book of hugs♥
lois blyth

<u>quote:</u> before engaging contact with another, hold a thought of love in your heart

U

unique

each unique Love is a
porition
of the universal
one love

☮♡☺♥✗

action: place your hands [on your] heart, close your eyes, + feel the love within you

song: ♥this is me♥ Keala Settle

book: ♥discipline is destiny♥ ryan holiday

quote: you are divine perfect + whole

☮ ♡ ☺ ♥ ★

visualize

the practice of seeing
love
leads to a life of
experiencing
love

<u>action</u>: for 1 minute close your
eyes + visualize love
flowing through your
veins

<u>song</u>: ♥pure imagination♥
Kathleen

<u>book</u>: ♥feeling is the secret♥
neville goddard

<u>quote</u>: when the heart +
mind are open
love is all we see

W

water

a universal gift
of
love

action: say ˹i love you˺ every time you use water

song: ♡let your love flow♡ the bellamy brothers

book: ♡be water, my friend♡ shannon lee

quote: a love like water transcends everything

☮♡＂ツ♡✳

X

x-ray vision

see the love in you
see the love in me
see the love in everybody

<u>action:</u> tap the third eye
+ say 'i see love'
10x daily

<u>song:</u> ♥i see love♥
♥jonas blue♥

<u>book:</u> ♥clarity + connection♥
yung pueblo

<u>quote:</u> when we see
with the heart
we see love

y
yoga

your   on   going adventure of love

action: balance on each
foot for 1 min

song: ♥om mani padme hum♥
ahha

book: ♥change your thoughts
change your life♥
wayne dyer

quote: the practice of
yoga
is the practice of
love

☮♡ :‿ ♥ ✱

Z

zeal

a life filled with
love
is created by
me

action: raise arms above the head + say "i love my life" 10x daily

song: ♥something good♥ ellen once again

book: ♥ soul boom ♥ rainn wilson

quote: love - the universal want, need + desire

☮ ♥ :) .♥ ✳

THE KEY TO SELF LOVE FROM A TO Z

A-Z	WORD	ACTION	CHECK
A	Attitude	Smile and say 'I choose Love' 10x :)	
B	Breath	Inhale Light, Exhale Love 10x :)	
C	Confidence	Smile and say 'I know I can' 10x :)	
D	Determination	Smile and say 'Love leads the way' 10x :)	
E	Exercise	15 Minute Answer workout with Trainer Joe :)	
F	Faith	Put hands on the hear and say 'I believe in Love' 10x :)	
G	Gratitude	Thank 1 or more strangers a day :)	
H	Help Others	Thank 1 or more people from you past who helped you :)	
I	Imagination	Imagine world love and tap your third eye 10x :)	
J	Joke	Say 'I am Joyful' 10x :)	
K	Kindness	Say something kind about yourself outloud :)	
L	Love	Say outloud 'I love my body' 10x :)	
M	Manifest	Write 'I create Love' 10x :)	
N	Nutrition	Before eating say 'Thank you body, I love you' :)	
O	Open - Minded	Tap the head and heart 10x :)	
P	Purpose	Say 'My purpose is to love and be loved' 10x :)	
Q	Quiet Time	15+ Minutes of yin yoga daily :)	
R	Read	Write 'I Love Myself' 10x :)	
S	Sleep	Draw 10 Hearts before bed :)	
T	Touch	Give yourself a hug for 5 breaths :)	
U	Unique	Place your hands on your heart, close your eyes, and fell the love within :)	
V	Visualize	1 minute close your eyes, and visualize love flwoing through your veins :)	
W	Water	Say 'I love you' everytime you use water :)	
X	X-Ray Vision	Tap the third eye and say 'I see Love' 10x daily :)	
Y	Yoga	Balance on each foot for 1 Minute :)	
Z	Zeal	Raise arms above the head and say 'I love my life' 10x daily :)	

i
Love
myself
+
i
♥
you too

www.ingramcontent.com/pod-product-compliance
Lightning Source LLC
Chambersburg PA
CBHW042322140726
48196CB00015B/697